She Says It This Way:

Tara K. Howe

She Says It This Way

Copyright © 2026 by Tara K. Howe
& Brian L. Jacobs,

Ann Arbor, Michigan USA
Published by Tofu Ink Arts Press. All rights reserved.
Book design by Brian L. Jacobs, Rashed, JLTY Atelier
ISBN: 978-1-958661-26-0

www.TOFUINK.com
A member of CLMP

Contents

Corset

The word corset is derived from the Old French word corps and the diminutive of body, which itself derives from corpus.

Full moon waning
Blood gone, corset
containing.

My spine has been crooked since I swung out of a tree.

As if I was the first monkey, or chimpanzee, and I fell to the ground, archangel beckoning. When I was in elementary school, I climbed a tree in the park across from our 76th avenue home, and as I gripped a branch above me to swing out and jump, I instead swung and cracked my tailbone on the stump of a limb removed, which catapulted me to the ground in such a state of white electric shock that I thought I was dying and said my first set of earnest goodbyes to the world. But then, upon not dying, stood up and went on. No longer the body I once was.

Today, and for the past week off and on, I've been wearing a corset and experimenting, not only with the length of time I can stand being bound, but also the resulting neurological sensations of sitting straight and tall. I used to have the time and take the time and not be a parent so did not feel guilty (at least not entirely) for having the time to go to the woods and bike for miles and hours until spent and returning for a beer and a gyro or an Ice treat. My spine, in addition to my limbs and my torso—my every fiber—was taut and capable of holding me upright. I did not collapse until after the birth of my third son and the marriage to his father.

I've been needing help to get upright again.

This corset is a light one, being, with plastic boning but quite solid and decidedly a corset, ordered from an online supplier specializing in this. It prevents a slouching in the gut and gives my nervous system constant suggestion of length and grace and style. Things I value, oddly, though I am quite raw, or have been. And so, without the endless hours of biking and hiking and camping and living with the woods, of instead being highly domesticated in a way that both serves and frightens, I find a societally constructed garment to contain and maintain and return to some way of prior being that I had in the trees.

I think about wounding. I read that Andy Warhol, after being shot, wore a corset. I feel better in this knowing. That another human, an artist, had also to turn to something more than himself to hold him up.

I think of wounding and how close it sounds to womb. How this has been my wounding. My entry point. My exit. My healing. My bane. My entire wisdom. And what it means to give it support. Protection. To hold in earnest. To hold at all.

I think of form. How the writing of this world is requiring form because it cannot yet be contained which is to say, there is no sense for others even though the beauty of a slug, say, is in its ooze and ability to understand the entire rhythm of its world through its fluid form.

Yet, how often ugly and unappealing to most is the slug and how there is no entry point for understanding its primordial rhythm unless a being can become fluid his or herself. In my hopes that others would take the shape of water, I overestimate the human condition and underestimate the power of form.

I write these forty-one word boxed prose poems attempting to keep this in mind.

Even water becomes ice to make itself known in its various permutations. Think snow. Think icicles. Think variation upon variation and what it means to be able to make and then recede from a shape.

I need not take so seriously the inability of myself or others to become water and osmose between us, and instead take seriously the constellated pattern of ice on a window as it presents itself over and over for different types of understanding.

Apply corset for hourglass, for leaning tower Pisa: define interior via scaffold's contraposition.

The Role of Molecular Gas in Galaxy Transition

I change too <fall into> constellation : : : become. Now winter, now snow, now no longer (volatile); not gasoline, nor CH20. Neither lighting nor embalming. [Still] the next ten years. What if I name myself my own star and revel in my constancy?

Saudi Neighbor *mt*DNA Permeability in Idaho Case Study

She was mango and date, silver platters of rice and chicken spiced. Gave (bones, heart, liver in a plastic bag) from lamb; bounty. Not *words* but *sensations*, and sometimes iPhone alphabet translations for things like doctor, and how to find babysitter.

Laceration of His Scalp Above the Temporal Bone as Examined by 6 yo Girl

Cherry is plum near charcoal, the underflesh milk white. *Blood* is not thought until pooling the temple, blinking eye <<<shutters her gaze wide>>> to children, *not children*, encircling the child. The rock has mass of moon / gravity untethered / at his feet.

Geothermal Effusion and Complex Multicellular Organisms

The place I go is crooning, crevassed in pine. *Magma* whispers succulent stone. I climb naked, amphibious, while cold crackles steam, tastes my skin. We make love, wet and me, then descend the trail in tan suede boots : become a doe.

Beta Testing: Maternal Display of Dominance in Multiparous Alpha Female

Inside my mother I carved a way : she took pins to a voodoo doll, breaking (as consequence) my good leg. If only there were *too many women* and we could birth ourselves forward into being / galaxies / vessels / wombs. Our own making.

Acoustic Impact of Coffee Percolating and Associated White Noise

If the strings of this steel guitar solo should puncture wounds already peeled . . . the piano
arrives next to unfurl, curl metal back from / and edges sharpened on : the white vinyl chair
reupholstered, the kitten drinking, silence of ovulation : this home song.

The Cumulative Effect of Stability in the Workplace

Filtered water, ice cubes, a sunny disposition to go with the large windows in the office. *Let's order you a company coat with a logo and won't you please stay?* (As though I wouldn't) / as though it hasn't been this hard.

Study of the Silkworm in Her Natural Habitat: A Prospectus

This time I don't turn back / go around / or fade. I take the gifts in front of me and keep being / the person I am / in the service of / so much more / than you can imagine. Infinite. I've come to / realize.

Mass Extermination Leads to an Array of Cognitive Impacts

But /// I'm still here in the [musk] [moist] [loess] of the Palouse. Eating my liver for its dreams. < Radiance > from the sunset shrouded his tales (some listen) but I speak now from the belly of a mountain : my grandfather come home.

Early Onset Visions : Alberta Case Study

One step. Two. Patent black shoes. Alice and the Ace *<I only came here to show you the way>* Red all roll. Baby put your best smile on (*this cheshire want*) / It's so easy to disappear *in* / the master's gone away.

Layering of Earth Rhythms in Bilingual Children's Realities

Je sais. Je sache. Je suis. J'ai (((sounds))) compiled of phylogenic branches that were ebbed from sand, guillotined through guttural // intonations // terse muscles to either side (this neck), head whipped <<north>> open wide. *Save me (from) isolation. Les mots* : mean everything.

Applied Astral Travel in the 21st Century

I fly at will and (used to be) outside of. Colors, sure, but shapes & gray. Pulse leads inside <<where I do nothing but observe>> your past, your now : our relatives. I did not choose this *yet* I know the way.

Coming of Age : American Adolescent Male and the Symbolic Role of Matricide

Hushed into crouch, gun laying across his lap @ Freeze Road. My son / man (becoming) waits << for her, the old one, hoof seismically rippled >> this second cartridge : nostrils bleed the lung. Her skin my wall, her skull. This / I asked of him.

Ontological Reflections Past Midday

Motherhood demands everything / I have never been as fierce. Her (deer) fleshed skull boils on the burner but (her) tallow travels in me, pulsing them (children), mine. Land. Even anger <<explosive>> soothes the 3pm, the too many days without / November sky.

The Tower of Babel Revisited from an Agnostic View

Au clair de la lune, mon ami Pierot . . . rock/man . . . and moon and a woman's name all in close succession; he needs a pen (a flying feather with ink) because the darkness consumes him. I cannot say in seven more words.

Even the Iliad Became Archaic

You did not think I could do this forever? The urgent need for form remains but my mother enters another eight rounds of electro-shock treatment. My co-worker turns out to be analogous to ex-husband. I drink Honey-Jack with the full moon.

Close Scrutiny of Predatory Behavior in [Domestic] Paradigm

The hawk is one of two that usually circles. Today she foots winter grass <<entirely attenuated>> near liquid skull off-boil (tallow, flesh, brain) and small scraps excised with pliers : left on deck : offer. Through glass, (her) Autonomic (Nervous) System, interprets. Us.

Spectral Archives : Post Lunar Swell

There was a moon (yesterday) that made me question [everything] // fold into my // mind. *Mamacita, won't you come out and* play? Today I understand what force ebbed within : I still yearn. (Three years ago, I was so young I granted every invitation.)

In the Alley There is Room for More

Bread and Pain. (Pain is bread in French). I see pain on the table. Discord in my h/earth. I want to cancel my meeting a half hour from now. I want often to cancel it all. *Remember : <<we exist>> to breathe.*

She Lives in a High Room Next Door to the Clouds That Watch Her Choose Among Tears and Photos

(I) select the (parts) of my life to frame. No longer needing to know [earth] through an open womb. Can I release the pounds I bear from carrying what is not mine? Now numbing ; no longer protecting --- instead of crave.

References (In Conversation With)

She Says by Vénus Khoury-Ghata, Translated by Marilyn Hacker. Graywolf Press. 2003.
The titles below are the titles of the prose poems I wrote while the italicized text is the phrase
from the poem in *She Says* that prompted the poem.

The Role of Molecular Gas in Galaxy Transition
The caravan that left the old town of Manama disappeared between Sirius and the Great Bear, 152.

Saudi Neighbor *mt*DNA Permeability in Idaho Case Study
*Arabic infusing its honey and its madness into French; the latter acting as a safeguard against over excitement
and side-slipping,* 159.

Laceration of His Scalp Above the Temporal Bone as Examined by 6 yo Girl
I'll tell you everything there were five pebbles / one for each continent, 5.
*When winter comes / she stands upright in its shadow / a pebble in her mouth to keep her words from freezing /
and her voice from speaking louder than the wind,* 155.

Geothermal Effusion and Complex Multicellular Organisms
Man and oak shared the same bark / the same age inscribed in the sapwood / and the same shadow, 25.

Beta Testing: Maternal Display of Dominance in Multiparous Alpha Female
There were too many women for too few seasons, 35.

Acoustic Impact of Coffee Percolating and Associated White Noise
She howls to frighten her own voice and make the water in the pond / / shudder, 39.

The Cumulative Effect of Stability in the Workplace
She only keeps those who flame up with her vine shoots, 93.

Study of the Silkworm in Her Natural Habitat : A Prospectus
Girls rich enough to have two buckets have the right to two lives, 145.

Mass Extermination Leads to an Array of Cognitive Impacts
...the woman who doesn't trust her lantern / has set the fireflies free, 47.

Early Onset Visions: Alberta Case Study
Their facades are painted blue to escape the bee's evil eye, 145.! 25

Layering of Earth Rhythms in Bilingual Children's Realities
Words she says are like rain everyone knows how to make / them, 23.

Applied Astral Travel in the 21st Century
In her dreams she thinks she is awake, 57.

Tara K Howe is a Canadian/American writer currently living in Moscow, Idaho. She speaks many languages — English. French. Science. Earth. Womb. Death. Birth. Body. Drum. — to explore the nature of somatic consciousness. "She Says It This Way :" began as an experiment in allowing form to serve as a support structure that might recondition the mind/body post-trauma. The project evolved into a micro-memoir, becoming its own container from which to study the ways grammar, sound, rhythm and syntax are ancestral—become home / of the earth. She has an MFA from the University of Idaho and her work has been published in several journals.